YOU GO GIRL!

A Journal to Get You There

KIM DOREN
CHARLIE JONES

**Andrews McMeel
Publishing**

Kansas City

ISBN: 0-7407-0878-3

Book design by Holly Camerlinck

To my nieces—Laura, Marie, Chloe, Alexa, and Cassandra. Thank you for filling my life with joy. I love you. The world is yours—You go girls!

KIM

To my niece Becky Jones Moore. Becky spent her life as a special teacher for special children until her time was cut short by cancer at the young age of thirty-nine. Her spirits never wavered during her eight-month battle with this deadly disease. Her rallying cry was always, "Come visit and bring a present." Becky, we miss you.

CHARLIE

CONTENTS

INTRODUCTION

There has never been a more exciting time to be a female athlete. The world is witnessing the exploding popularity of women's sports. From the members of the U.S. national soccer team to the individual stars of professional tennis, female athletes are everywhere—on television, magazine covers, and cereal boxes. Opportunities are expanding at all levels, and women are taking advantage of them to experience the joys of competition.

Participating in athletics is incredibly empowering. You learn how to set goals, be disciplined, gain confidence, face defeat, and celebrate victory. Best of all, the journey is filled with great moments and meaningful friendships.

This journal is designed to help prepare you for your journey in life, not just your journey in sports. It poses questions to help you better understand yourself. You'll discover your passions, your motivations, your strengths, your weaknesses, and ultimately, your values. By writing down your answers to the various questions, you'll be one step closer to becoming the person you want to be.

Write it down, make it happen. Such advice sounds simple, but it really works. By expressing your feelings and ideas on paper, your dreams and goals become clearer. You'll be surprised how much more you can accomplish by making your thoughts tangible.

How you approach this journal is entirely up to you. You may choose to skip around to different chapters. You may even want to start from the back and work your way forward. You may decide to share some of your answers with a friend, a coach, or your parents. Or you may prefer to keep all your answers private. You must decide what works best for you.

You'll find it valuable to occasionally review what you've written. This will enable you to chart how you've progressed or changed. It will also reenergize you. Remember, this is not a test; there are no right or wrong answers. Use this journal to help you reflect on your life, on what matters to you, and on where you want to go. But most important, enjoy your journey.

ABOUT ME

Today's Date _May 6, 2002_

Name _Jacqueline Lee Platt_

Age _17_

Address _99 Sunset Hill Rd_

Phone _203 - 804-5899_

Parents _Kevin & Michele Platt_

Sisters and brothers _George Platt_

Pets _1 springer spaniel named Isabell_

Best friends _Kelly DiBisceglie Jen Marino-San_

School I attend and my grade level _____

Branford High School Grade 12

Favorite subject _Possibly English & History_

Favorite teachers _Mr. Petela & Mr. Ogren_
Mrs. Wright

Sports I play Diving; TENNIS

Favorite sport Tennis

Favorite team B.HS. Girls Tennis (so far)

Hobbies Riding Bicycles, learning how to talk, & spell, hiking, Swimming, I have many garments for my feet, body, & limbs, reading (hope for it to become one), Smiling

What I want to be doing in ten years

SOMETHING

- Graduated sacred Heart
- Traveled out of the country (or Books)
- Read at least 50 books

ONE

FIND
YOUR
PASSION

"Each of us has a fire in our hearts for something. It's our goal in life to find it and to keep it lit."

MARY LOU RETTON,
Olympic gymnastics champion

WHAT
do you love to do the most?

I tend to think a lot but it really does not get me anywhere. Only recently and a few years before that I became voliourable to others persuasion when all I should be in touch with is mine. I went hiking recently but have ~~just learnt~~ allways enjoyed being outside and not worrying about sooooooooo much. I wish I could agee with Evelyn. I sim enjoy running.

> "I just love the feeling of running. I love the challenge of it."
>
> EVELYN ASHFORD,
> *Olympic track champion*

WHY does doing your favorite activity make you happy?

Being outside allows me to often not care so much about... me. The only thing that matters is the fact that I am doing something without completely acknoledguing what it is. However I used to be able to do that wherever I was but now I seem to sweet while I had conversation. I am nervous but I choose not to deal with it. I would rather sweet and smell then constantly worry

WHAT
are your talents?

_____

_____

_____

_____

_____

_____

_____

_____

_____

_____

_____

WHAT
are your dreams?

_____

_____

_____

_____

_____

_____

_____

_____

_____

_____

_____

"You need to have dreams; everything starts with a dream."

SHEILA CORNELL-DOUTY,
Olympic softball champion

_____

_____ ■

LIST
all the things you like to do.

_____

_____

_____

_____

_____

_____

_____

_____

_____

_____

"Never do it to please some-   _____
one else. It has to be yours."
PEGGY FLEMING,   ——————————— ■
Olympic figure skating
champion

LIST
all the things you dislike doing.

_____

_____

_____

_____

_____

_____

_____

_____

_____

_____

_____ ■

DO you prefer individual sports or team sports? Why?

_____

_____

_____

_____

_____

_____

_____

_____

_____

_____

"The whole team concept is
such a joy for me . . . we're
all like sisters and best friends.
That's a huge part of the
passion for me."

JULIE FOUDY,
World Cup soccer star

WHAT *activity makes you lose all sense of time?*

_____

_____

_____

_____

_____

_____

_____

_____

_____

_____

_____

HOW can others help you find your passion?

_____

_____

_____

_____

_____

_____

_____

_____

_____

_____

_____

_____

WHO are the people in your life (family, coaches, friends) who have encouraged your dreams and talents?

_____

_____

_____

_____

_____

_____

_____

"What's fun for me as a coach is to watch someone who has a love for diving, who's just doing it because it's a blast to fly through the air."

MICHELE MITCHELL-ROCHA,
University of Arizona diving coach

LIST *those moments in life when you've felt most fulfilled.*

_____

_____

_____

_____

_____

_____

_____

_____

_____

_____

"You can only be great at something that makes you happy."

_____

_____ ■

LIZ DOLAN,
sports executive

WHAT *is your passion?*
When and how did you discover it?

_____

_____

_____

_____

_____

_____

_____

_____

_____

_____

_____

_____

Final Thoughts . . .

_____

_____

_____

_____

_____

_____

_____

_____

_____

"I get a mental high, a physical
high, and an emotional high
because I love what I'm doing.
I have a passion for it, and
when all three come together
in certain matches, there's no
better feeling in life."

CHRIS EVERT,
tennis champion

TWO

MAKE A COMMITMENT

"I do know that I train harder than anyone else in the world. Last year I was supposed to take a month off, and I took three days, because I was afraid that somebody out there was training harder. That's the feeling I go through every day—Am I not doing what somebody else is doing? Is someone out there training harder than I am? I can't live with myself if someone is."

MARION JONES,
world champion sprinter

WHAT are your goals for this week? This month? This year?

_____

_____

_____

_____

_____

_____

_____

_____

_____

_____

"The people who are really going to do something are the ones who set goals for themselves."

DEBI THOMAS, *world champion figure skater*

WHAT would you like your life to be like in five years? What do you hope to be doing in five years?

_____

_____

_____

_____

_____

_____

_____

_____

_____

_____

_____ ■

DO you have goals that you share with others (such as with your team or with a friend)? What are they?

_____

_____

_____

_____

_____

_____

_____

_____

_____

_____

_____

DO you have both big "pie-in-the-sky" goals and little, daily goals? What are they?

_____

_____

_____

_____

_____

_____

_____

_____

"One reason I have so many smaller goals is that even if my big goal doesn't happen, I've still achieved so much along the way, I don't feel the loss."

SHANNON MILLER,
Olympic gymnastics champion

WHAT type of preparation do you need to accomplish your goals?

_____

_____

_____

_____

_____

_____

_____

_____

_____

_____

"A lot of people want to achieve success, but only a few are willing to pay the price."

VIVIAN STRINGER,
Rutgers basketball coach

WHAT *actions are you taking to achieve your goals?*

_____

_____

_____

_____

_____

_____

_____

_____

_____

_____

_____

_____ ■

LIST *the commitments you have made. List the commitments you still have to make.*

_____

_____

_____

_____

_____

_____

_____

_____

_____

_____

_____ ■

WHY *are these commitments important to you?*

_____

_____

_____

_____

_____

_____

_____

_____

_____

_____

"Don't just fit in with the crowd; try to be extraordinary."

KERRI STRUG,
Olympic gymnastics champion

WHAT sacrifices have you made to keep these commitments?

_____

_____

_____

_____

_____

_____

_____

_____

_____

_____

"You might be making sacrifices now, but the fact is you are making an investment in yourself."

GABRIELLE REECE,
beach volleyball star

HOW *do you deal with missing out*
on a lot of fun things?

_____

_____

_____

_____

_____

_____

_____

_____

_____

_____

_____

_____ ■

WHAT *does **total commitment** mean to you?*

_____

_____

_____

_____

_____

_____

_____

_____

_____

_____

"The difference between a good athlete and a top athlete is the top athlete will do the mundane things when nobody's looking."

_____

_____

_____ ■

SUSAN TRUE,
educator

WHAT *are you totally committed to and why?*

_____

_____

_____

_____

_____

_____

_____

_____

_____

_____

_____

_____

_____ ∎

Final Thoughts . . .

_____

_____

_____

_____

_____

_____

_____

_____

_____

_____

_____

"A true champion works hard and never loses sight of her dreams."

DOT RICHARDSON,
Olympic softball champion

THREE

GO
FOR
IT

"In life, not just in sports, if you don't try, you cannot know what you can do."

MANON RHEAUME,
Canadian hockey star

LIST *your greatest victories.*
List your worst defeats.

_____

_____

_____

_____

_____

_____

_____

_____

_____

_____

_____

_____

WHAT *do you learn from winning?*
What do you learn from losing?

**"A winner's strongest muscle
is her heart."**

CASSIE CAMPBELL,
Canadian hockey Olympian

HOW *do you regroup when you are losing?*

_____

_____

_____

_____

_____

_____

_____

_____

_____

_____

"You have to want it more and be hungrier than your competition."

LYN ST. JAMES,
race car driver

WHAT *have been your toughest challenges?*

_____

_____

_____

_____

_____

_____

_____

_____

_____

_____

_____

_____ ■

WHO has helped you become a better competitor? How?

_____

_____

_____

_____

_____

_____

_____

_____

_____

_____

_____

_____

HOW do you deal with pressure?

_____

_____

_____

_____

_____

_____

_____

_____

_____

_____

_____

**"Worry about the last mile
when you get there."**

NANCY RIEDEL,
track and field coach

WHY *do you compete?*

_____

_____

_____

_____

_____

_____

_____

_____

_____

_____

"I'm not a person who wants to win at any price, but I want to be the best I can, in everything I do."

SYLVIE BERNIER,
Canadian Olympic diver

HOW do you feel when you're competing? Do you **hate to lose** more than you **love to win**?

_____

_____

_____

_____

_____

_____

_____

_____

_____

_____

_____ ■

HAVE you ever been in the zone?
How does it feel?

_____

_____

_____

_____

_____

_____

_____

_____

_____

_____

_____

_____

HOW *do you stay focused on the challenge at hand?*

_____

_____

_____

_____

_____

_____

_____

_____

_____

_____

"It's the mental part of the game that separates the winners from the losers."

_____

_____

CHRIS EVERT,
tennis champion

LIST *some sports you would like to try and explain why.*

_____

_____

_____

_____

_____

_____

_____

_____

_____

_____

"I don't want to look back on my life and say, 'What if?'"

ANNIE MEYERS
DRYSDALE,
basketball All-American

WITH all the sports and activities in life you'd like to try, what's keeping you from **going for it?**

_____

_____

_____

_____

_____

_____

_____

_____

_____

"The only person who can stop you from reaching your goals is you."

JACKIE JOYNER-KERSEE,
Olympic track champion

Final Thoughts . . .

_____

_____

_____

_____

_____

_____

_____

_____

_____

_____

"If it's something you really
want to do, something that
you love with all your heart,
do it. You do things for you,
not for someone else."

STACEY SWAYZE,
professional jockey

FOUR

SHE GOT NEXT

"I think as far as women in sports, we still have a long way to go. It's not about sport, it's about how to compete in our society. It's not being left out of the sandbox. We all have to play together and respect each other, and the sooner we learn to, the less discrimination there'll be."

DONNA DE VARONA,

Olympic swimming champion

HOW would you feel if you were told girls can't do that?

_____

_____

_____

_____

_____

_____

_____

_____

_____

_____

"A lot of people think girls cannot do this. I want girls to see that they can."

FABIOLA DA SILVA,
champion in-line skater

WHAT *do you do when someone tells you **girls can't do that?***

_____

_____

_____

_____

_____

_____

_____

_____

_____

_____

_____ ■

DO women have the same opportunities as men in sports at your school? What are the differences?

_____

_____

_____

_____

_____

_____

_____

_____

_____

_____

_____

WHAT *could be done to improve the athletic experience for women?*

_____

_____

_____

_____

_____

_____

_____

_____

"For girls to be really
successful . . . they have to
learn from boys and men
about exercising their
strength and power. Sports
are a perfect vehicle for
teaching that."

M. BURCH TRACY FORD,
educator

HAVE *you ever had to face a negative stigma about being a female athlete? Explain.*

_____

_____

_____

_____

_____

_____

_____

_____

"It's okay to be competitive, aggressive, and ornery, and still be feminine."

AMY VAN DYKEN,
Olympic swimming champion

WHAT *are the positive aspects of being a female athlete?*

_____

_____

_____

_____

_____

_____

_____

_____

_____

_____

_____

_____ ■

DO you prefer a female or a male coach? Why?

"I think men should be given
the opportunity to coach
women if they choose, and
women should be given the
opportunity to coach men if
they choose."

SHERYL SWOOPES,
Olympic basketball star

DO you prefer watching women's or men's professional sports? Why?

_____

_____

_____

_____

_____

_____

_____

_____

_____

_____

_____

_____

HOW can we be sure that girls have the same opportunities in sports as boys do?

_____

_____

_____

_____

_____

_____

_____

_____

_____

"When you change the hearts and minds of people, and match legislation, then you've arrived."

BILLIE JEAN KING,
tennis champion

WHICH *women athletes or coaches have shown you that women can achieve great things? How did they show you?*

_____

_____

_____

_____

_____

_____

_____

_____

_____

_____

_____ ■

HOW *do you encourage girls who are younger than you are?*

_____

_____

_____

_____

_____

_____

_____

_____

_____

"One of the best things
about the sports experience
is that it teaches women to
compete. To openly seek
victory and to dare to win."

MARIAH BURTON
NELSON,
author

WHAT advice would you give to the next generation of athletes?

_____

_____

_____

_____

_____

_____

_____

_____

_____

_____

_____

_____ ■

Final Thoughts . . .

_____

_____

_____

_____

_____

_____

_____

"There's a negative stigma that goes with being a female athlete—that you can't be feminine and still be an athlete. I don't think that's true. I think you can be a woman on or off the court. But you can also be a great competitor on or off the court. I don't think there's anything wrong with mixing the two."

REBECCA LOBO,
WNBA star

FIVE

NEVER GIVE UP

"Success is never giving up, never letting yourself get lazy, and never allowing yourself to surrender."

KRISTINE LILLY,
World Cup soccer star

DESCRIBE *a time when you didn't give up. What motivated you to keep going?*

_____

_____

_____

_____

_____

_____

_____

_____

_____

**"The harder you work, the
harder it is to surrender."**

PAT SUMMITT,
*Tennessee
basketball coach*

HAVE *you ever quit? Why or why not? Do you have any regrets? Explain.*

_____

_____

_____

_____

_____

_____

_____

_____

_____

_____

_____ ∎

SHOULD *you always finish what you start? Why or why not?*

_____

_____

_____

_____

_____

_____

_____

_____

_____

_____

_____

_____

HOW do you stay positive and motivated when things are going against you?

_____

_____

_____

_____

_____

_____

_____

"**Winners take bad breaks and use them to drive themselves to be that much better. Quitters take bad breaks and use them as a reason to give up.**"

NANCY LOPEZ,
LPGA star

NAME someone who inspired you to persevere through difficult times and explain how.

_____

_____

_____

_____

_____

_____

_____

_____

_____

_____

_____

HOW do you force yourself to keep going when you are losing by a lot?

_____

_____

_____

_____

_____

_____

_____

_____

_____

"In the middle of a race, when I'm dead tired, I ask myself, 'How tough can you be?' "

_____

_____

_____ ∎

CHRIS WITTY,
Olympic speed skater

HOW *have you encouraged teammates or friends not to give up?*

_____

_____

_____

_____

_____

_____

_____

_____

_____

_____

_____

HOW
do you define success?

_____

_____

_____

_____

_____

_____

_____

_____

_____

_____

"Success is knowing in your heart that you gave everything you had. Win or lose, you gave it your all and had some fun in the process."

MIA HAMM,
World Cup soccer star

DO you play to win, or do you play not to lose? Explain.

_____

_____

_____

_____

_____

_____

_____

_____

_____

_____

_____

_____

WHAT *excuses have you used when you have lost?*

_____

_____

_____

_____

_____

_____

_____

_____

_____

_____

_____

"You can't measure success if you have never failed."

STEFFI GRAF,
tennis champion

HOW do you feel when you don't give up?

_____

_____

_____

_____

_____

_____

_____

_____

_____

_____

_____

WHAT is more important to you, the journey or the outcome? Why?

_____

_____

_____

_____

_____

_____

_____

_____

_____

_____

"What matters is knowing I did absolutely everything I could possibly do to win. The results are less significant than the effort."

KELLY WILLIAMS,
national champion fencer

Final Thoughts . . .

_____

_____

_____

_____

_____

_____

_____

_____

_____

"I'm not glad that I fell, but
I'm glad I fought for it, that
I didn't stomp off like a
baby. I hope that at these
Olympics people remember
me for how hard I tried,
not how great I did."

NICOLE BOBEK,
Olympic figure skater

SIX

FACE YOUR FEARS

"When I'm up on the hill I have moments of fear. I'm human and when I look at a course there are times when I say, 'Wow, that's hairy,' and I'm afraid of that part of the course. But what you do is face that fear with the task at hand and then you don't have the fear, because fear is nonproductive. Just wheels spinning."

PICABO STREET,
Olympic skiing champion

WHAT
are your fears?

_____

_____

_____

_____

_____

_____

_____

_____

_____

_____

_____

_____

DO
you fear competition? Explain.

_____

_____

_____

_____

_____

_____

_____

_____

_____

_____

_____

"I was always chased by the fear of being beaten."

SHIRLEY STRICKLAND,
Australian track star

HAVE *you ever been afraid of losing? Explain.*

_____

_____

_____

_____

_____

_____

_____

_____

_____

_____

"A champion is afraid of losing. Everyone else is afraid of winning."

BILLIE JEAN KING,
tennis champion

HAVE you ever been afraid of winning? Explain. Is it okay to be afraid? Explain.

_____

_____

_____

_____

_____

_____

_____

_____

_____

_____

_____

HOW and when has fear been helpful to you?

_____

_____

_____

_____

_____

_____

_____

_____

_____

_____

_____

_____

IF *you give 100 percent and lose, how do you handle that?*

_____

_____

_____

_____

_____

_____

_____

_____

_____

_____

"To me, never trying feels a lot worse than failing."

DEBI THOMAS,
*world champion
figure skater*

HOW do you let fear bring out the best and the worst in you?

_____

_____

_____

_____

_____

_____

_____

_____

_____

_____

"It's okay to be scared, but don't let it dictate your action."

MICHELLE AKERS,
World Cup soccer star

HOW
do you overcome your fears?

DO
you ever fear failure? Why?

_____

_____

_____

_____

_____

_____

_____

_____

_____

_____

_____

"Fear of failure drives me competitively."

NANCY LOPEZ,
LPGA star

WHEN
have you felt fearless?

_____

_____

_____

_____

_____

_____

_____

_____

_____

_____

_____

_____

_____

_____

WHAT preparations can you make to face your fears?

_____

_____

_____

_____

_____

_____

_____

_____

_____

_____

"The butterflies were there but they were flying in formation."

SHEILA CORNELL-DOUTY,
Olympic softball champion

HOW will facing your fears
prepare you for life ahead?
Why is this important?

_____

_____

_____

_____

_____

_____

_____

_____

_____

_____

_____ ■

Final Thoughts . . .

_____

_____

_____

_____

_____

_____

_____

_____

_____

"Everyone is afraid. Everyone wants to be awesome and look awesome. Everyone is really afraid of getting out there and not being good. That's the challenge. What singles out successful athletes is that they do it anyway even though they are terrified."

AIMEE MULLINS,
track star

SEVEN

BELIEVE IN YOURSELF

"You've got to believe in yourself.
The ones who believe in themselves
the most are the ones who win."

FLORENCE GRIFFITH-
JOYNER,
Olympic track champion

WHAT
do you like about yourself?

_____

_____

_____

_____

_____

_____

_____

_____

_____

_____

_____

"You can always find something good within you."

CHARMAINE HOOPER,
Canadian soccer star

WHAT *would you like to change about yourself?*

_____

_____

_____

_____

_____

_____

_____

_____

_____

_____

_____

_____ ■

WHAT are your strengths? What are your weaknesses?

_____

_____

_____

_____

_____

_____

_____

_____

_____

_____

_____

_____

WHAT *are your most important achievements? What do they mean to you?*

_____

_____

_____

_____

_____

_____

_____

_____

_____

_____

_____ ■

WHAT *gives you confidence?*

_____

_____

_____

_____

_____

_____

_____

_____

_____

_____

_____

_____

"There's a fine line between being conceited and having confidence in yourself. Conceit is thinking you can do it without hard work and perseverance."

CAROL HEISS JENKINS, *Olympic figure skating champion*

DO you ever lack confidence?
When and why? What do you do to
overcome self-doubts?

_____

_____

_____

_____

_____

_____

_____

_____

_____

_____

_____

_____ ■

WHAT
makes you feel good about yourself?

_____

_____

_____

_____

_____

_____

_____

_____

_____

_____

_____

_____

_____

WHO has been a big believer in you? In what way?

_____

_____

_____

_____

_____

_____

_____

_____

_____

_____

"My mother taught me very early to believe I could achieve any accomplishment I wanted to. The first was to walk without braces."

WILMA RUDOLPH,
Olympic track star

WHAT

will it take for you to be a champion?

_____

_____

_____

_____

_____

_____

_____

_____

_____

"Your physical body can only
take you so far. It's your
emotional body, the confidence
you have, that takes you to a
higher level."

AIMEE MULLINS,
track star

IS *a personal best good enough for you if it doesn't land you in first place? Explain.*

_____

_____

_____

_____

_____

_____

_____

_____

_____

_____

_____

_____

HOW *do you control your emotions before a competition?*

_____

_____

_____

_____

_____

_____

_____

_____

_____

_____

_____

_____

DO
you use visualization? Explain.

_____

_____

_____

_____

_____

_____

_____

_____

_____

"Before every pitch I throw, I
see where I want it to go.
I've already thrown the ball
in my mind, and it was a
good pitch."

ILA BORDERS,
professional baseball pitcher

Final Thoughts . . .

"I always believed I can beat
the best, achieve the best. I
always see myself in the top
position."

SERENA WILLIAMS,
U.S. Open tennis champion

EIGHT

OVERCOME OBSTACLES

"I've learned you can overcome the biggest setbacks. I focus on turning the negatives into positives. If you want it and you dream about it . . . there's nothing that's going to stop you."

CHRIS WITTY,
Olympic speed skater

WHAT has been your biggest disappointment? How did you feel afterward?

_____

_____

_____

_____

_____

_____

_____

_____

_____

_____

HOW *do you come back from disappointment?*

_____

_____

_____

_____

_____

_____

_____

_____

_____

_____

"You face adversity all the time. I accept what lies ahead and then I do my best to make it through."

KRISTINE LILLY,
World Cup soccer star

_____

_____

_____ ■

WHO has helped you deal with disappointment? How did they help?

_____

_____

_____

_____

_____

_____

_____

_____

_____

_____

_____ ■

HOW *do you feel when you overcome an obstacle?*

_____

_____

_____

_____

_____

_____

_____

_____

_____

"Happiness is derived from achievement and achievement is derived from overcoming something that at first might have been difficult."

MICHELE MITCHELL-
ROCHA,
Olympic diver

_____

_____

_____

_____ ■

HAVE you ever failed? What did you learn from failure?

_____

_____

_____

_____

_____

_____

_____

_____

_____

_____

_____

_____

"You've always got to be aware of why you don't win; otherwise, you'll keep losing."

LAYNE BEACHLEY,
world surfing champion

WHEN *you're facing defeat, explain the risks you will take in order to win.*

_____

_____

_____

_____

_____

_____

_____

_____

_____

_____

_____

_____ ∎

WHAT do you do after a loss? How does this differ from what you do after a win?

_____

_____

_____

_____

_____

_____

_____

_____

_____

_____

_____

DO *you believe that your time will come? What if it doesn't?*

"All you can do is your best.
If you've done that, there's
nothing else you can give
and you should be proud of
yourself."

JOY FAWCETT,
World Cup soccer star

HOW *do you lift your spirits when you're down?*

_____

_____

_____

_____

_____

_____

_____

_____

_____

"I try to have a positive
attitude when life throws a   _____
curve. I have been so lucky
in my life that I try to never   _____
feel sorry for myself."
                                     _____ ∎
MIA HAMM,
World Cup soccer star

HOW *do you help your teammates after a loss? How do they help you?*

_____

_____

_____

_____

_____

_____

_____

_____

_____

_____

_____

WHAT
are the obstacles facing you?

_____

_____

_____

_____

_____

_____

_____

_____

"Too often our biggest
limitations are the ones we
place on ourselves or allow
others to place on us."

JEAN DRISCOLL,
marathon wheelchair champion

HOW *do you intend to overcome your obstacles?*

_____

_____

_____

_____

_____

_____

_____

_____

_____

_____

_____

_____ ∎

Final Thoughts . . .

_____

_____

_____

_____

_____

_____

_____

_____

"Failure usually turns into a
great learning experience. It's
a chance to learn how to
persevere and it fires you up
to give more the next time
around."

CLAIRE CARVER-DIAS,
*Canadian synchronized
swimmer*

NINE

EMBRACE YOUR COMPETITIVE SPIRIT

"I hope to raise my daughter not to be a spectator, not to be on the sideline. I want her to be on the playing field, no matter what it is. I want her to experience the joy of competition and of sport."

LISA RAINSBERGER,
Boston Marathon winner

WHEN *are you competitive? Do you have to win at everything? Why or why not?*

_____

_____

_____

_____

_____

_____

_____

_____

_____

_____

_____

SHOULD *you be competitive all the time? Explain.*

_____

_____

_____

_____

_____

_____

_____

_____

_____

"On the water I'm very
aggressive. I go for it. I
don't hold back. But off the
water I'm very easygoing."

KELLY MOORE,
champion windsurfer

WHAT *do you like about competition? What don't you like about competition?*

_____

_____

_____

_____

_____

_____

_____

_____

_____

_____ ∎

HOW *do you feel when you win?*
How do you feel when you lose?

_____

_____

_____

_____

_____

_____

_____

_____

_____

_____

_____

_____ ■

"Winning—it's better than breathing!"

AMY VAN DYKEN,
asthmatic Olympic swimmer

WHAT *do you like about practice?*
What don't you like about practice?

_____

_____

_____

_____

_____

_____

_____

_____

_____

_____

_____

_____ ■

EXPLAIN *how you feel when you're in the middle of a great competition.*

"The happiest I've ever been in my life is when I'm on the court."

NANCY LIEBERMAN-CLINE,
basketball champion

WHAT *is an example of good sportsmanship?*

"Sportsmanship is not just
about being nice . . . it's
about realizing that you
could not compete without
an opponent and that she has
the same goals as you."

STEPHANIE DEIBLER,
softball player

ARE you a good sport? How would you like to change?

_____

_____

_____

_____

_____

_____

_____

_____

_____

_____

_____

_____ ∎

HOW important are the friends you make along the way? Is it difficult competing against friends?

_____

_____

_____

_____

_____

_____

_____

_____

_____

_____

_____ ∎

WHAT type of people do you most like to compete against? Why?

_____

_____

_____

_____

_____

_____

_____

_____

_____

_____

"You've got to look for
tough competition. You've
got to want to beat the best."

GRETE WAITZ,
_New York City Marathon
champion_

ARE you consumed with winning or with being the best you can be? Explain.

_____

_____

_____

_____

_____

_____

_____

_____

_____

_____

_____

H O W *do you feel about yourself as a competitor?*

_____

_____

_____

_____

_____

_____

_____

_____

_____

_____

"I'm mostly competitive within myself. It's not always a matter of having to beat everyone."

SONDRA VAN ERT,
Olympic snowboarder

Final Thoughts . . .

_____

_____

_____

_____

_____

_____

_____

_____

"If it's the last shot, I want
the ball. I don't necessarily
want to score, but I want the
ball so I can make the right
decision whether to score or
whether to dump it off to
someone else."

DAWN STALEY,
*Olympic basketball
gold medalist*

TEN

BE A ROLE MODEL

"The term *role model* is too often applied to people whose accomplishments we admire. They've won a medal or made a million dollars or are a good surgeon. These things are admirable. But true role models are those whose character has set an example."

LIZ DOLAN,
sports executive

HOW *important are role models?* *Explain.*

_____

_____

_____

_____

_____

_____

_____

_____

"I remember the impact people whom I looked up to had on me when I was young. It can really make a difference . . . because it gives you a little more incentive."

KERRI STRUG,
Olympic gymnast

LIST

the ten people you most admire.

_____

_____

_____

_____

_____

_____

_____

_____

_____

_____ ■

HOW *have your parents and siblings influenced you?*

_____

_____

_____

_____

_____

_____

_____

_____

_____

"My dad has taught me I
could do anything I set my
mind to, so I always have."

_____

CRISTEN POWELL,
drag racer

WHO is the most influential person in your life with respect to athletics? Why?

_____

_____

_____

_____

_____

_____

_____

_____

_____

_____

_____

_____ ■

SHOULD *athletes be role models? Why or why not?*

_____

_____

_____

_____

_____

_____

_____

_____

_____

_____

"Don't aspire to be like me. Be better. Shoot higher."

FLORENCE GRIFFITH-JOYNER,
Olympic track champion

LIST *your favorite athletes and the reasons why you like them.*

_____

_____

_____

_____

_____

_____

_____

_____

_____

_____

_____

_____ ■

WHO are your favorite coaches? Why?

_____

_____

_____

_____

_____

_____

_____

_____

_____

_____

_____

_____

A R E *you a good team player?*
Why or why not?

_____

_____

_____

_____

_____

_____

_____

_____

_____

"A team is like little matches
that together create a big
fire."

CLAIRE CARVER-DIAS,
Canadian synchronized
swimmer

ARE you a role model? If yes, do you enjoy it? If no, would you like to be one? Explain.

_____

_____

_____

_____

_____

_____

_____

_____

_____

"If I can have some influence on a child's life, that's one of the greatest honors anybody could ever have."

KELLY WILLIAMS,
national fencing champion

HOW would you like to be remembered by your teammates and competitors?

_____

_____

_____

_____

_____

_____

_____

_____

_____

_____

_____ ∎

Final Thoughts . . .

_____

_____

_____

_____

_____

_____

_____

"As people teach their children about competition, and
the ups and downs and how
to deal with them, I guess I
can stand to be a role model.
They can say, 'She didn't win
but she's still standing up tall
and smiling and loving her
sport.' "

MICHELLE KWAN,
Olympic figure skater

ELEVEN

THERE'S MORE TO LIFE THAN WINNING

"The medals don't mean anything and the glory doesn't last. It's all about your happiness. The rewards are going to come, but the happiness is just loving the sport and having fun performing."

JACKIE JOYNER-KERSEE,
Olympic track champion

IS *winning the most important thing in sports? Why or why not?*

_____

_____

_____

_____

_____

_____

_____

_____

_____

_____

**"Winning is not the end-all,
be-all; performing to the best
of your ability is."**

SYLVIE BERNIER,
Canadian Olympic diver

BESIDES *winning, what are other things that matter when you play sports?*

_____

_____

_____

_____

_____

_____

_____

_____

_____

_____

_____

_____ ■

DO you feel pressure from others to always win? What do they say or do to make you feel that way?

_____

_____

_____

_____

_____

_____

_____

_____

_____

_____

_____

NAME *an experience in sports that you enjoyed that had nothing to do with winning or losing.*

———————————————————

———————————————————

———————————————————

———————————————————

———————————————————

———————————————————

———————————————————

"Ten years from now you're not going to remember where you placed in a competition but you're going to remember the friends you made along the way."

————————————

————————————

————————————

———————————— ■

MICHELE MITCHELL-
ROCHA,
Olympic diver

WHEN *have you lost but still felt like a winner? Why?*

_____

_____

_____

_____

_____

_____

_____

_____

_____

_____

_____

_____

DOES *how you feel about yourself depend on your wins or losses? Why?*

_____

_____

_____

_____

_____

_____

_____

_____

_____

"Who I am as a person is not dependent on whether I win or lose."

KELLY WILLIAMS,
national fencing champion

RANK the aspects of your life in order of importance. (For example: family, school, church, sports, health, friends, work.)

_____

_____

_____

_____

_____

_____

_____

_____

_____

_____

_____

DO *you have balance in your life?*
If not, what areas of your life need
more attention?

_____

_____

_____

_____

_____

_____

_____

_____

_____

_____

"What's after the Olympics?
Life."

JOAN BENOIT
SAMUELSON,
Olympic marathon champion

WHAT *are your favorite memories about playing sports?*

_____

_____

_____

_____

_____

_____

_____

_____

_____

_____

"There's a purity about
women's sports that's
refreshing."

JULIE FOUDY,
World Cup soccer star

IF *you had one wish, what would it be?*

_____

_____

_____

_____

_____

_____

_____

_____

_____

_____

_____ ■

"If you try hard and you have
fun and you're a good sport,
you're a success no matter
what the score. I think that's
equally true at the Olympic
level. You could be perfectly
prepared. You could do
absolutely everything right.
You could run the best race
of your life and other people
could beat you. That doesn't
mean you are not a success."

NANCY DITZ,
Olympic marathoner